# An Old Red Hat

Story by Jane Langford
Pictures by Anni Axworthy

Ada had a nest.
"What have you got there?" asked Mum.

"One... two... three eggs in a nest,"
said Ada.

"That's not a nest!" said Mum.
"That's my old red hat!"
"I'm going to sell the eggs at the market," said Ada.

Ada got on the bus to go to market.

A boy on the bus saw Ada.
"What have you got there?" he asked.

"One... two... three eggs in a nest,"
said Ada.

"That's not a nest!" said the boy.
"That's an old red hat!"

A lady on the bus saw Ada.
"Let me see. What have you got there?" she asked.

"I have got one... two... three eggs in a nest," said Ada.

"I'll give you three pennies for the eggs," said the lady.

Ada got off the bus at the market.

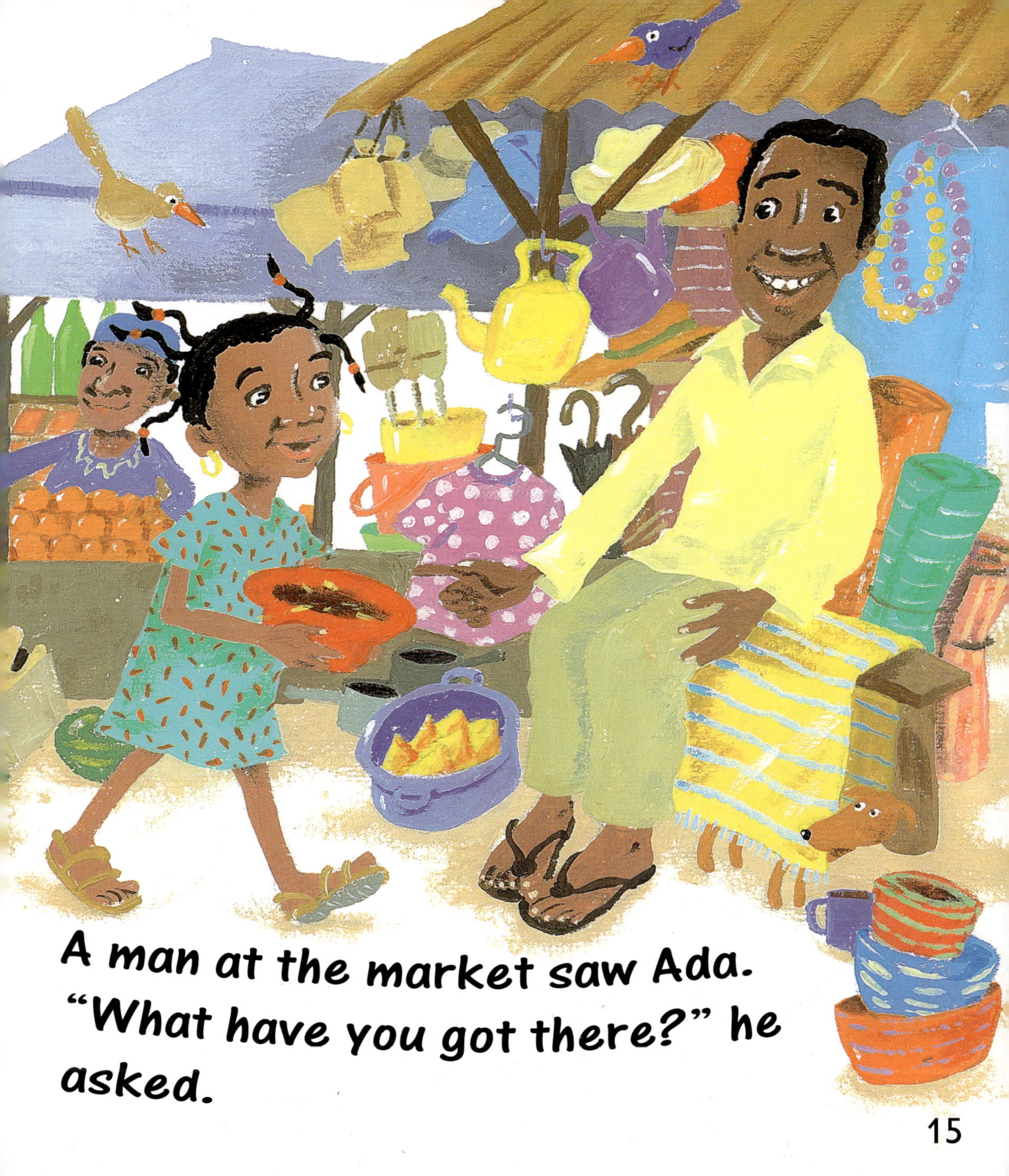

A man at the market saw Ada.
"What have you got there?" he asked.

"One... two... three pennies!" said Ada. "What can I get with three pennies?"

"Give me the three pennies and you can have this," said the man.

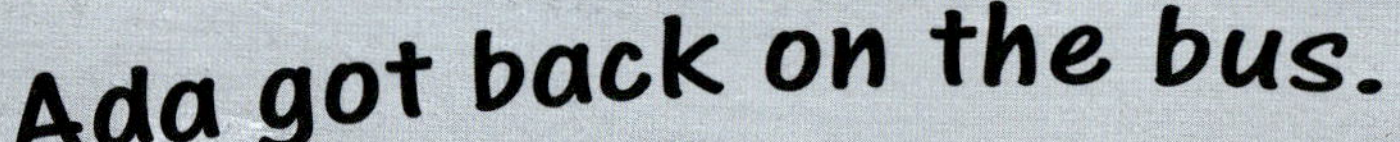
Ada got back on the bus.

A girl on the bus saw Ada.
"What have you got there?" she asked.

Ada shook her head and smiled.

She got off the bus and went home.

Mum saw Ada.
"What have you got there?" she asked.

"It's for you," said Ada.

It was a **new** red hat!

"Thank you, Ada!" said Mum.